BASS BUILDERS

6-String Bass

BY DAVID GROSS

All calculations set to one side

The inevitable descent from Heaven

A visitation of memories and a seance of rhythms invades my house

My Head, and the world of my mind

— Arthur Rimbaud

To Nancy August,

Where does one begin?

PLAYBACK+
Speed · Pitch · Balance · Loop

To access audio visit:
www.halleonard.com/mylibrary

Enter Code
4601-7791-6920-6545

ISBN 978-0-7935-8371-3

HAL•LEONARD®
CORPORATION

7777 W. BLUEMOUND RD. P.O. BOX 13819 MILWAUKEE, WI 53213

Visit Hal Leonard Online at
www.halleonard.com

CONTENTS

INTRODUCTION

Fourteen years ago I was walking down 48th Street, the instrument mecca of NYC, and in the window of one of the music stores was a strange looking bass with six strings! Immediately I began to think of the extraordinary range of this instrument and the possibilities of two-handed tapping, chords, and melodies. I walked in the store, played it for a bit, and two days later purchased what was the first of ten six-string basses. I knew I had found my voice!

This instrument met with some strange looks from many producers and players back then, but has now become an accepted part of the bass player's arsenal.

This book has come from my desire to illustrate the myriad possibilities this instrument holds in terms of range, flexibility, and style. I have included play-along tracks to help you with the many examples included in this book.

If you have played a four- or five-string bass and want to now experiment with a six string, or if you want to tackle this instrument right from the start, this book is for you. I will explain chords, scales, and techniques for soloing, and there will be many exercises to help you facilitate your new learning.

So without further ado, grab your bass and let's get started!

THE PLAY-ALONG TRACKS

The play-along tracks were a lot of fun to record. I have put the exercises on the left side, the drums in the center, and the harmony line on the right. I used a Warwick Streamer 1 to record the tracks and the drum programs were created by Steve Dwire on a Akai MPC 3000. We used an Alesis ADAT to record and, as technology has improved, so has the quality of the home studio.
I hope you enjoy these recordings and find them useful in your studies!

The audio portion was recorded and mixed at SMD Music Group, New York, NY
All drums and percussion by Steve Dwire using the Linn/Akai MPC–3000
Special thanks to Roger Linn at Roger Linn Design, Ben Cano at Akai, and "Rose" at International Music Corp.
Steve Dwire can be reached via e-mail at: zzdom@earthlink.net

ACKNOWLEDGMENTS

I would like to thank the following people who helped in the creation of this work:

Charlie Banacos
Ken Bebensee—KB Guitars
Mike Brown—Dana B. Goods and Warwick Basses
The staff at Hal Leonard Corp.
Steve Dwire—for his killer drum programs
Dave Flores—Carvin Musical Products
Gerry Griffin—Eventide
Larry Hartke—Hartke Systems
John Medic—Passport Systems (Makers of Encore Software—used in the creation of this work)
Greg Romano—D'Addario Strings
Roy and Joan Ruzika—Performance Solutions
Happy Traum—Homespun Tapes
(look for the *Mastering the Six-String Bass* video)
Larry Ullman—Euphonic Audio

CHAPTER 1
THE "BASSICS"–SCALES AND ARPEGGIOS

Major Scales

Learning any instrument requires you to memorize the fingerings of scales and their chord tones (arpeggios). Like any language, you need to learn both vocabulary and grammar before you can speak effectively. This chapter will give you the tools to negotiate effortlessly up and down the neck of your bass.

If you are comfortable on a four-string bass and are switching to the six string, you have probably encountered some of the patterns we will be using. With the inclusion of the low B and high C strings, new and more economical ways of playing are now available.

Let's take the G major scale and play it in one position as if we are playing a four-string bass:

Fig. 1

If we subscribe to a "one finger per fret" philosophy, we are limited to an octave and a 4th.

Starting on the G with the six-string bass, we are now able to go as high as the 7th, almost two full octaves.

Fig. 2

If we take that same pattern and transpose it into D major starting on our low B string, we can now finger two octaves and a ♭3rd (and up to the major 3rd with a stretch).

Fig. 3

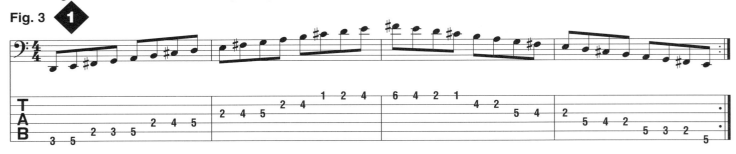

This added flexibility helps in two very distinct ways:

- When reading a piece of music, you have more confidence by not having to shift positions.
- When performing live, this can be translated into *entertaining the audience* and not looking at your hands.

Remember: *all* the exercises you learn in D major are applicable to *all* other scales, arpeggios, and patterns. To really understand the material in this book takes focus, discipline, and transposition through all keys. *All keys are easy keys when you are fluent in them!*

Here are three more ways to finger a two-octave D major scale:

Fig. 4

Notice how the first fingering pattern lets us move more comfortably into the third octave?

Fig. 5

When I move over the entire fingerboard, I like to think in terms of traversing the neck using a combination of vertical and diagonal moves. A good way to visualize this concept is with the *major seventh arpeggios.* Here are three different fingerings:

Fig. 6

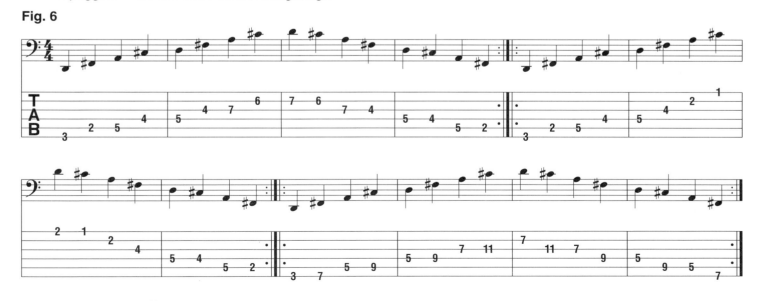

Here is the same arpeggio using three octaves in a constant diagonal movement:

Once you become familiar with these fingerings, I suggest breaking up the variations in different groupings to help get the patterns under your fingers and into your ears.

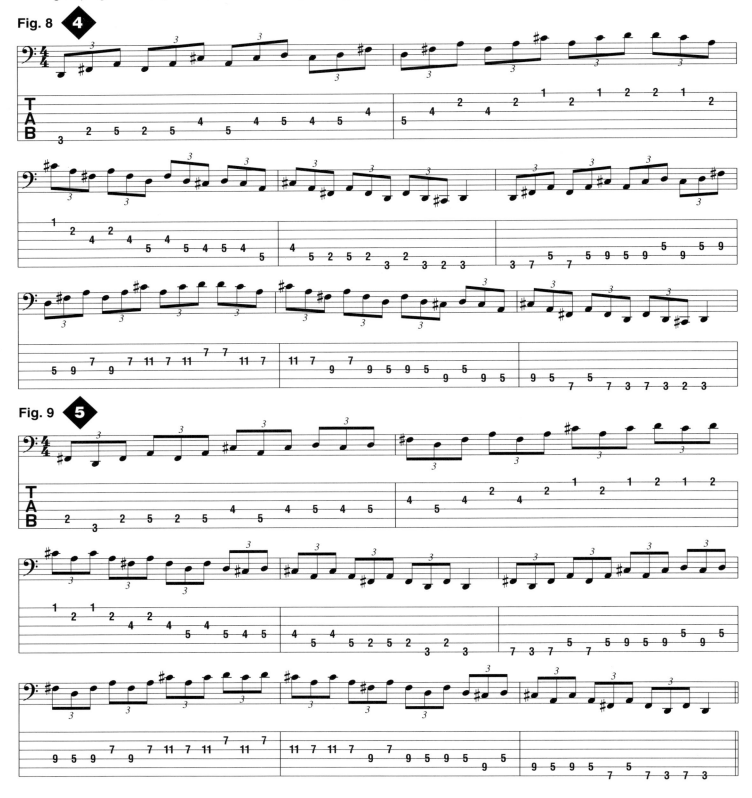

Another important exercise to help you internalize arpeggios is the inversion. *Inversions* are simply permutations of the original chord. Here is a Dmaj7 arpeggio and all of its inversions. Pay attention to the sound of the chord as its starting note changes. The fingering I chose takes you up the neck one way and down another.

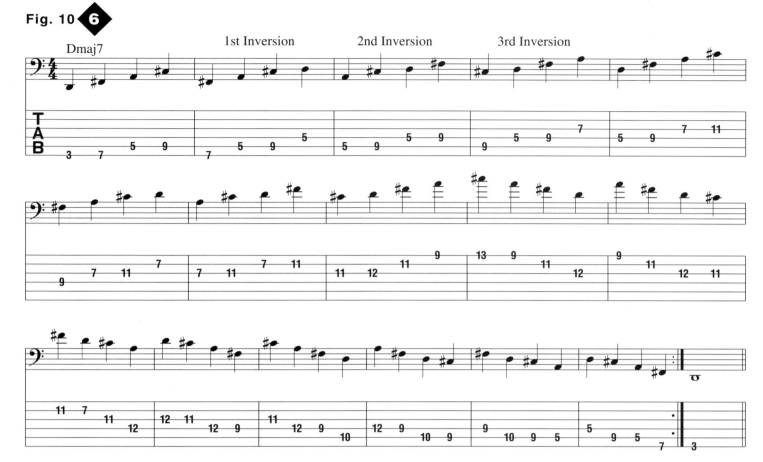

It is important to remember that while we are illustrating technique and theory, we are also addressing ear training. Learning the sounds and relationships of all the intervals (up and down) will help you to reproduce them on your instrument. There are no tempo markings for these exercises because I want you to find a speed you are comfortable with and then slowly increase it.

When we view the major scale as the reference point for all other scales in Western music (see chart in the Appendix) it becomes obvious we should start memorizing the sounds of this scale first!

Here is the D major two-octave scale in thirds. Bear in mind it is important to learn the sounds of these intervals in both their *ascending* and *descending* patterns.

Here is the same pattern with a different fingering. It is important to devise as many fingerings as possible to really get to know your neck.

Fig. 12

Let's try 4ths:

Fig. 13 8

Fifths in one position create this fingering:

Fig. 14 9

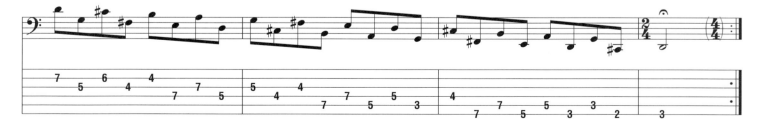

Sixths create an interesting sound:

Fig. 15

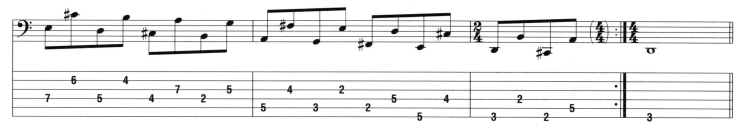

Fingerings for 7ths are a little unusual.

Fig. 16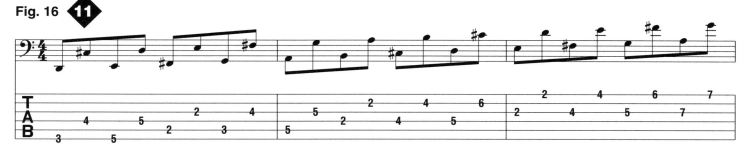

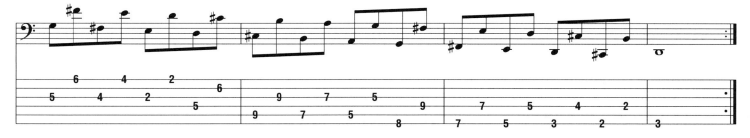

Here we have octaves.

Fig. 17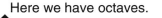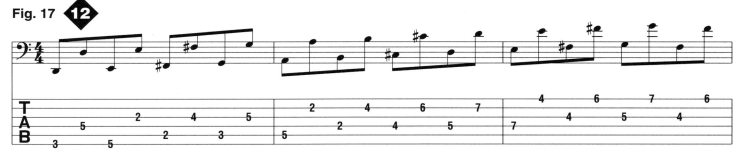

Above the octave we can finger the 9ths, which are just the second degree of the scale up an octave.

Fig. 18 13

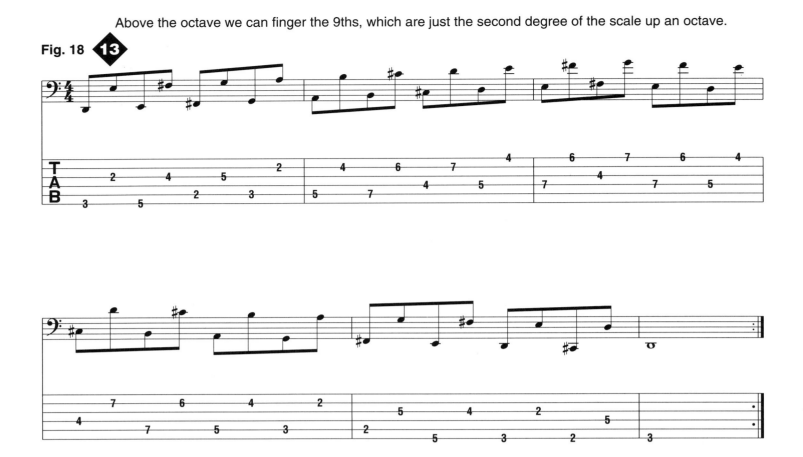

Tenths are a recognizable sound—the third an octave up.

Fig. 19 14

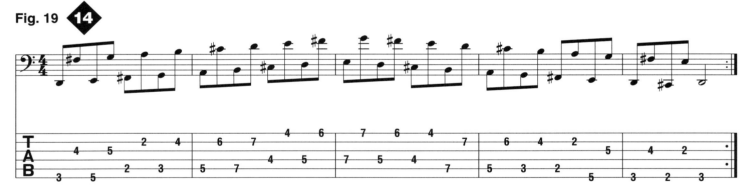

As we increase the size of the intervals, pay strict attention to your picking hand in regard to the string skips. I like to use either my thumb and first finger or my first and second fingers, but it is really up to you to figure out what is most comfortable.

Modes

The easiest explanation of the modes would be to view them as extensions of the major scale. If you start your D major scale on the second degree of the scale, you create the E *Dorian mode.* This is a minor mode and includes a ♭3 and ♭7.

Fig. 20: E Dorian mode

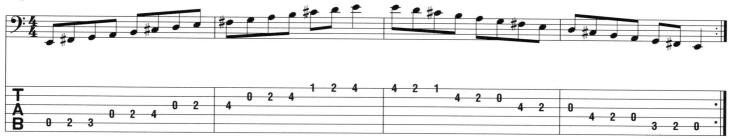

Starting on the third degree of the scale we have the F♯ *Phrygian mode.* This minor mode features a ♭2 (or ♭9), ♭3, ♭6, and ♭7.

Fig. 21: F♯ Phrygian mode

The fourth degree of the scale starts the G♯ *Lydian mode.* This mode is similar to the major scale with one difference: the fourth note is raised (♯4 or ♯11).

Fig. 22: G Lydian mode

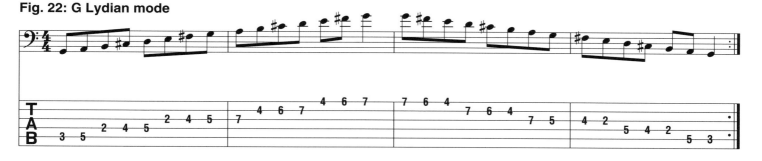

The fifth degree of the scale gives us the A *Mixolydian mode* which is the dominant scale. This too is similar to the major scale, except for the ♭7.

Fig. 23: A Mixolydian mode

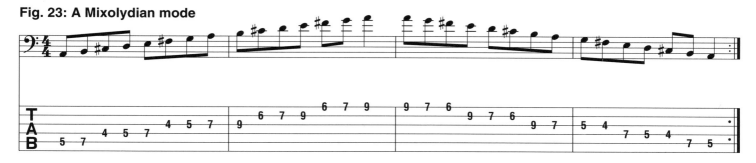

The sixth degree creates the B *Aeolian mode,* also known as the *natural* or *relative minor scale.* This mode features a ♭3, ♭6, and ♭7.

Fig. 24: B Aeolian mode

The seventh degree of the major scale creates the C♯ *Locrian mode,* also called the *half-diminished mode.*

Fig. 25: C♯ Locrian mode

I have always felt that, as a bassist, one of my roles is to articulate the harmony by creating bass lines that follow the chord progression. This is easiest to see in a trio situation with guitar and drums. I make certain when the guitarist is soloing, both the players involved and the audience do not get lost. One of the ways I can do this in a melodic way is by looking at arpeggios as two-octave scales in thirds.

Here are the arpeggios created from the modes.

Fig. 26: E Dorian arpeggio 15

Fig. 27: F♯ Phrygian arpeggio 16

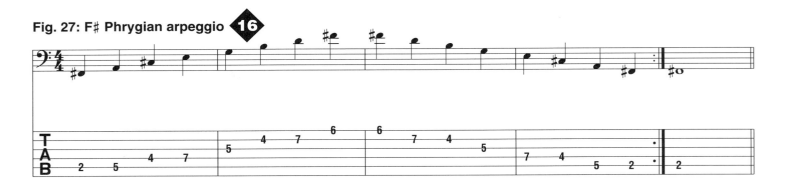

Fig. 28: G Lydian arpeggio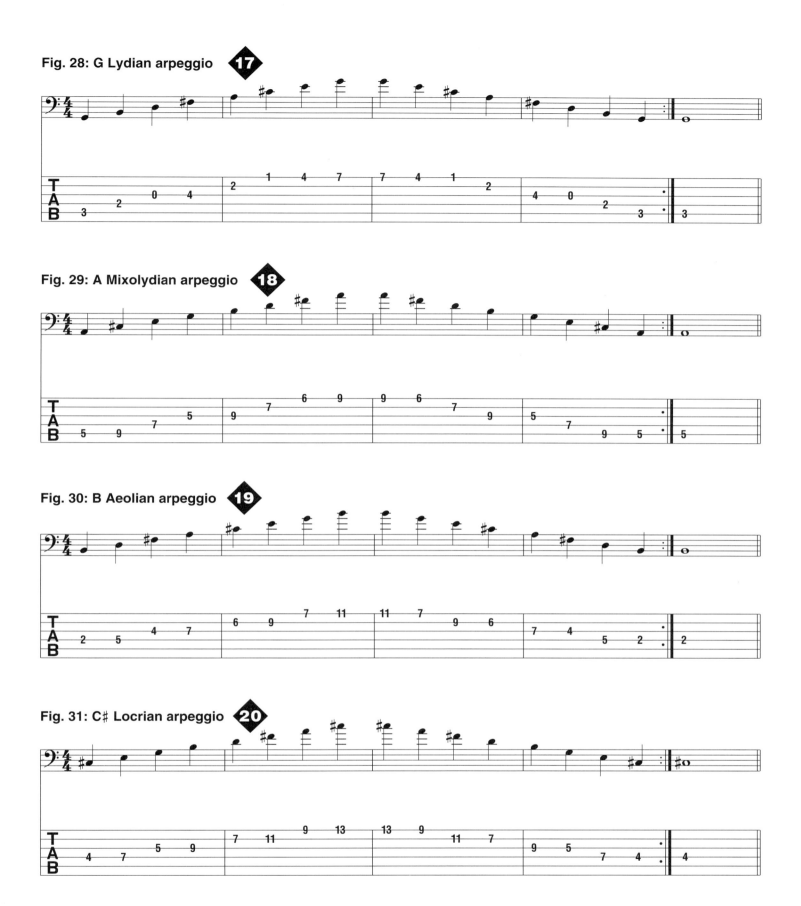

Fig. 29: A Mixolydian arpeggio

Fig. 30: B Aeolian arpeggio

Fig. 31: C# Locrian arpeggio

Remember: the exercises we used to learn the major scale and its modes can be applied to these modes and arpeggios in all keys! These principles can also be applied to any scale you encounter.

To help familiarize yourself with other scales, check out the chart in the Appendix that spells out a number of scales frequently used in music today.

CHAPTER 2
CHORD FORMS

Major Chords

Two of the things that attracted me to the six-string bass were the fact that I could play chords in a higher register without sounding muddy, and I could create chords that had complex voicings. In this chapter we will tackle chords, theory, and their application. Let's go back to that Dmaj7 chord.

Fig. 32

We can use two different fingerings when we play this arpeggio as a chord.

Fig. 33A 21   **Fig. 33B** 22

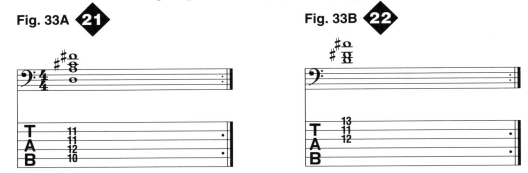

In the second example I eliminated the 5th. In a number of the following chords I eliminate the 5th because I feel it does not tell us a lot about a chord—unless it is a ♭5 or ♯5. Sometimes the 5th can make things muddy.

Inversions of this chord are also available and can create interesting springboards for songwriting.

Fig. 34 23

I can eliminate the 5th when I play the maj7 with the 9th (a maj9 chord).

Fig. 35 24

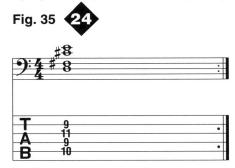

And I can also play the 9th chord without the 7th (this is sometimes referred to as an add9 chord).

Fig. 36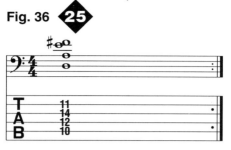

When it comes to the maj7 with an added 11th, I will usually exclude the 3rd or the 5th and I will always sharp the 11th!

Fig. 37

When I play the maj13 chord, I eliminate the 3rd and add a 9th. This chord uses the root, 5th, 9th, and 13th.

Fig. 38

Here we have a maj13 with the 3rd, major 7th, and 13th (no 5th).

Fig. 39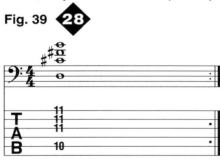

Here is an example of the various major forms combined in a four-measure phrase.

Fig. 40

 Now try playing fig. 40 with just the rhythm track.

cont.

Minor Chords

We can approach minor chords the same way. Let's take a look at an Em7 chord, which is the ii7 chord in the key of D.

Fig. 41

There are two comfortable fingerings for this chord—one without the 5th.

Fig. 42A 30

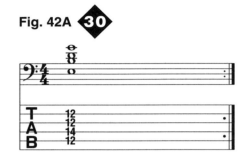

Fig. 42B 31

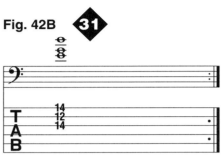

When we add the 9th, we have two possibilities. Here is the Em7♭9. This chord is a part of the melodic minor scale *(see the Appendix)*. There is no 5th in this voicing of the chord.

Here is the Em9 chord. This chord voicing also has no 5th.

Fig. 43 32

Fig. 44 33

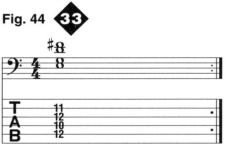

In my last video, *Mastering the Electric Bass,* I wrote a song, "For Courtney," that utilizes this chord form in A and adds the ♯5th and 6th as well.

Fig. 45 34

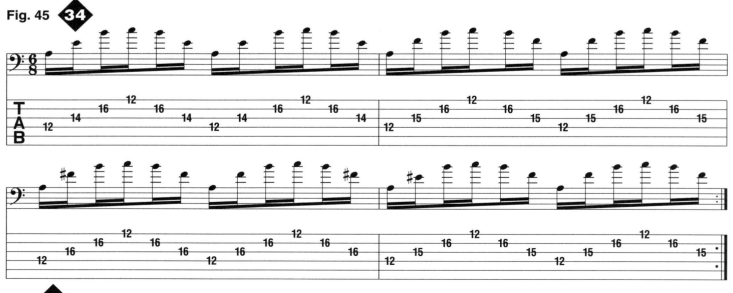

34 **cont.** Now try playing fig. 45 with just the rhythm track.

The Em11 chord typically replaces the 5th with the 4th (11th).

Em13 includes both the ♭7th and the 13th (6th).

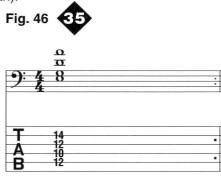

Fig. 46

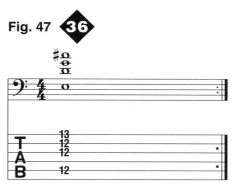

Fig. 47

Take a look at this chord progression arpeggiating four minor chords.

Fig. 48

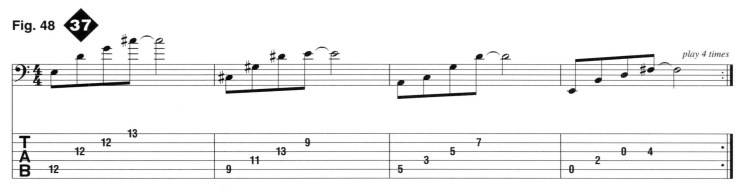

 Now try playing fig. 48 with just the rhythm track.

cont.

Remember: any minor chord will use these same fingerings. Only the root will change! This means the Bm7 (the vi7) will look like this (and the Cm11 in Fig. 49E):

Fig. 49

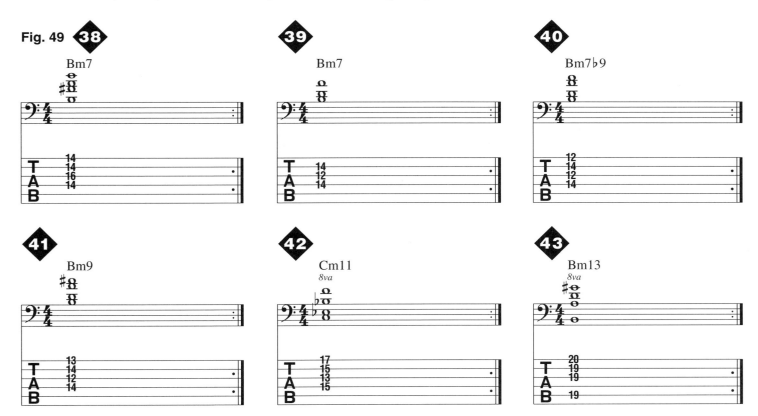

Dominant Chords

The dominant seventh chord is an important element in your arsenal of chords. Take a look at the A7 fingerings. The first and second examples show the same fingering, with the second one eliminating the 5th.

Fig. 50

Here is a blues progression using two of the fingerings.

Fig. 51

We can add an F#m7 chord and a Bm7 chord to create a I–vi–ii–V turnaround.

Fig. 52

Now try playing fig. 52 with just the rhythm track.

cont.

Here are the three 9th chord possibilities—A7♭9, A9, and A7♯9.

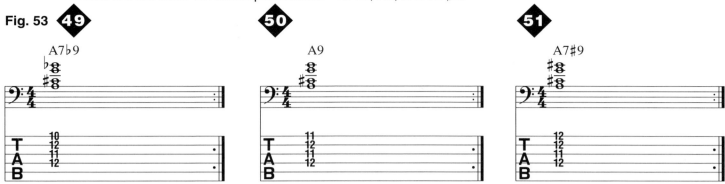

I like the sound of the A7♯11 chord. It leaves you waiting for a resolution.

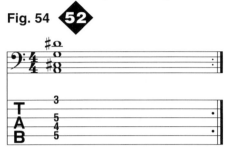

The A7(13) fingering takes you over five strings.

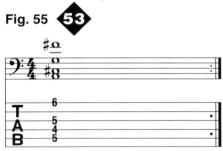

Here is a pattern that combines chord tones from the chords above. Remember to use your ears to pick out the intervals that sound musical to you.

 Now try playing fig. 56 with just the rhythm track.

cont.

Another chord in the dominant family is the *augmented chord.* This chord uses a ♯5th. The augmented chord has a flavor of anticipation.

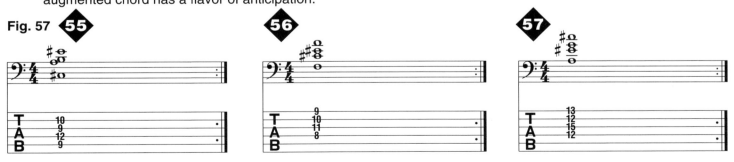

Diminished Chords

The diminished seventh chord is fun because each chord is equivalent to four chords! This means that any of the four notes can be the root of the chord. Here is the fingering I like to use.

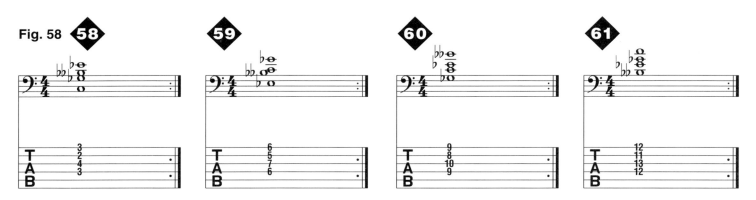

We can include this chord in our blues progression. See how nice it sounds in the sixth measure of the progression.

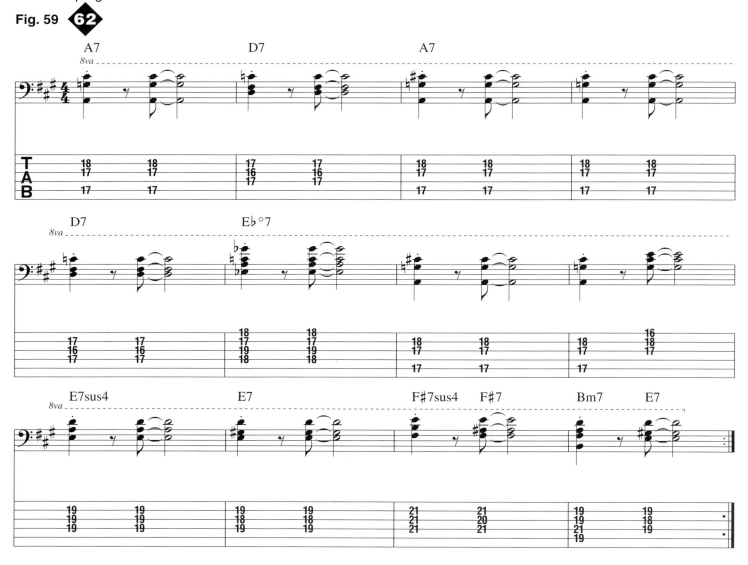

62 Now try playing fig. 59 with just the rhythm track.

cont.

Here is an interesting pattern utilizing both chords and licks.

Fig. 60

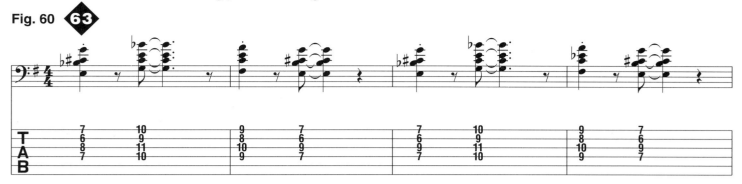

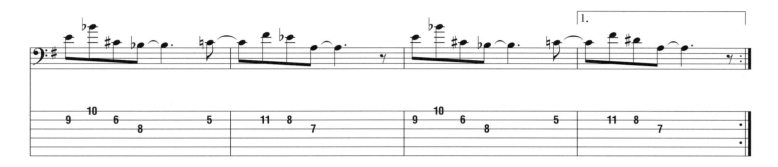

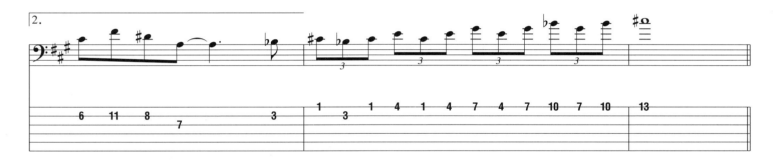

63 cont. Now try playing fig. 60 with just the rhythm track.

These *chord forms* are only a starting point. I suggest experimenting with other fingerings to help you create and find other sounds.

CHAPTER 3
TWO-HANDED TAPPING

Concepts for Two-Handed Tapping

The range of the six-string bass always reminded me of a keyboard; when I think of two-handed tapping I view it the same way. Simply think of the left hand as the bass end and the right hand as the high end. To help you gain facility of the right hand, I have devised a few dexterity exercises that will develop your chops and will hopefully spur you on to greater discoveries. You will use all four fingers on the right hand. These exercises actually help your plucking ability too!

This first exercise mirrors the left-hand version of the major scale. Play it slowly and evenly. Don't worry if it feels awkward at first because you will be performing tasks that are unfamiliar to your muscle memory. In time you should be up to speed.

Fig. 61: Major scale 64

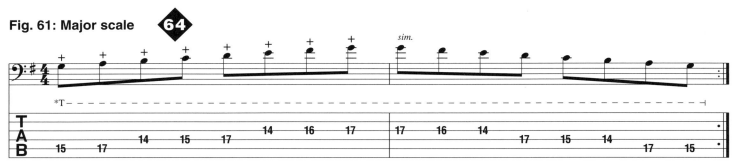

* Tap with right hand index finger.

This next exercise incorporates 3rds with the major, Dorian, Mixolydian (dominant), augmented, and diminished scales.

Fig. 62: Major scale 65

Fig. 63: Dorian mode 66

Fig. 64: Mixolydian mode 67

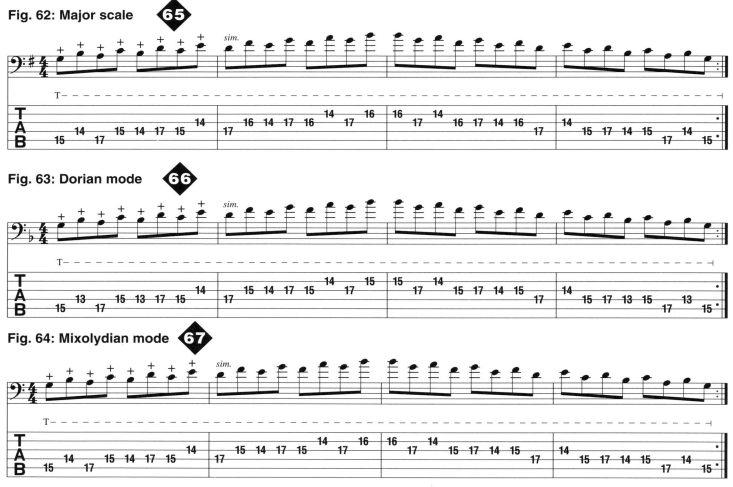

Fig. 65: Augmented scale ◆68◆

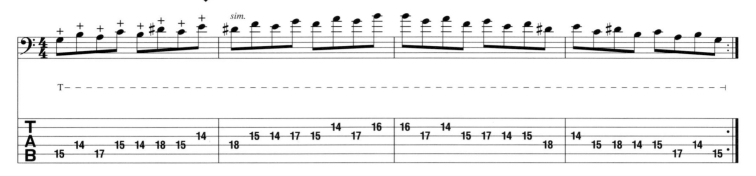

Fig. 66: Diminished scale ◆69◆

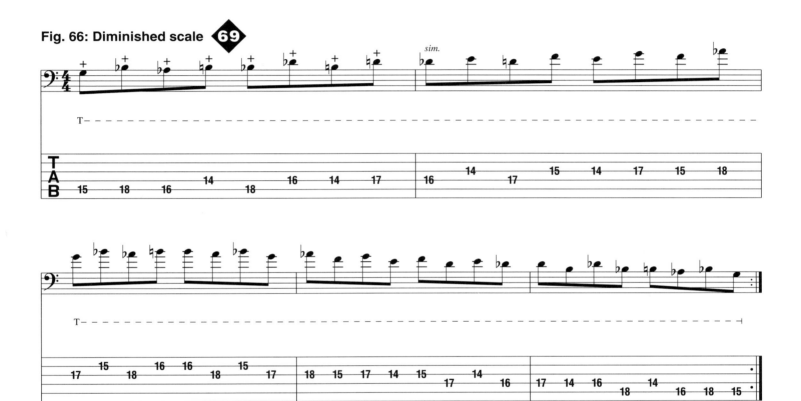

Remember: any scale can be used with these exercises. Try 3rds with the harmonic and melodic minor scales, the whole tone scale, etc.

This exercise uses two notes at once. When you tap these notes, do it as close to the fret as possible. It will sound more distinct this way.

Fig. 67: Major scale ◆70◆

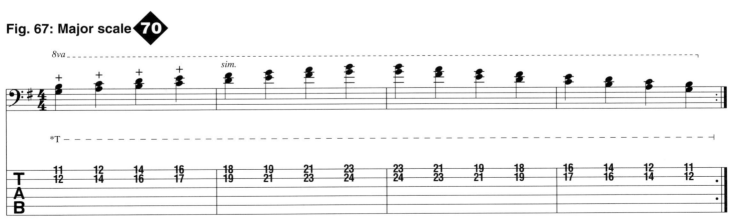

* Tap with right hand 1st and 2nd or 1st and 3rd fingers.

Theory for Two-Handed Tapping

ver the next seven figures, we are going to build a song with two-handed tapping. Let's concentrate on the left hand for now. Try and tap as close to the fret as possible. Not only will you get a better sound, but if you tap on a fretless à la Les Claypool, your intonation will be dead on. I like to spread out my voicings when I arpeggiate chords. My favorite left-hand intervals are 5ths and 6ths.

Fig. 68

* Left hand hammers on from "nowhere."

cont.

I also like to work with octaves. Keeping a good pulse is key. Because I am more familiar with left hand fingerings, I try to put the left hand on "automatic pilot" so I can then concentrate on my right hand. (Obviously it is the reverse for you lefties!) Here is a basic pattern that keeps a solid groove.

Fig. 69

This next example is a busier version of the last. As you can see, when tapping there are no open strings.

Fig. 70

Here is a pattern to try with your right hand.

Fig. 71

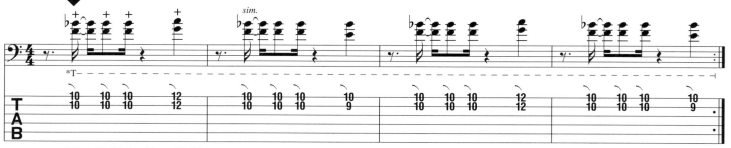

* Tap with right hand 1st and 2nd fingers.

From a theoretical point of view, when you put figs. 70 and 71 together, the first chord is a Gm7 with the left hand playing the bass note and the right hand tapping the ♭7th and ♭3rd. The second chord is a Gsus with the right hand tapping the root and the 4th. The third chord is a Gm6 with the right hand tapping the 6th and the ♭3rd.

Now let's try another grouping:

Fig. 72

And now for the right hand part. The fingerings are the same but the chord theory is different.

Fig. 73

Putting figs. 72 and 73 together, we have an E♭sus chord with the left hand pedaling the E♭ and the right hand tapping a 4th and a ♭7th. The second chord is an E♭ power chord with the 5th and the root in the right hand, and the third chord is an E♭7 chord with the right hand tapping the 3rd and the ♭7th.

To finish this song, we have one last pattern. Here is the left hand pattern:

Fig. 74

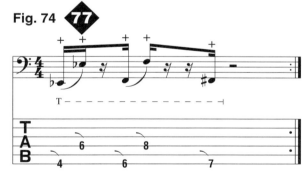

Here is the right hand—which is E♭sus, F7 with a 5th and a ♭7th, and an F♯7 with a 5th and a ♭7th.

Fig. 75

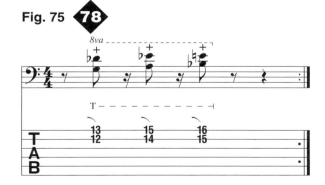

The next step is to play both of these patterns together! As a bassist, I find it easier to play a simple left hand bassline and a more complex right hand melody. Start slowly and bring the tempos up to speed. There is an example on the play-along track.

 Figs. 69-75 with the right- and left-hand patterns played together.

 Now try playing this song with just the rhythm track.
cont.

Let's take a look at a more melodic and flowing pattern. With my left hand, I will play a root-5th pattern.

Fig. 76

With my right hand I will play a repetitive pattern that can be called an *ostinato.* This pattern remains constant while the left hand pattern changes, creating different chords. With the E in the bass we have an Em9 chord with a 9th, ♭3rd, and ♭7th. With the C in the bass we have a Cmaj9#11 chord with the 5th, 9th and #11th, and with the D in the bass we have a D7add11 chord with a 3rd, 4th (11th), and root.

Fig. 77

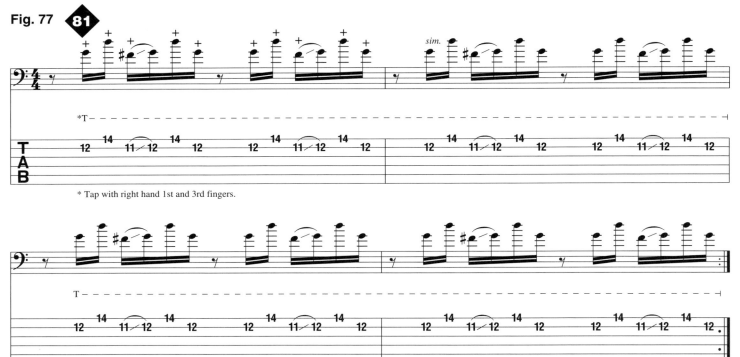

* Tap with right hand 1st and 3rd fingers.

Once again, let's try and put these patterns together.

 Figs. 76 and 77 played together.

 Now try playing figs. 76 and 77 with just the rhythm track.
cont.

As you can see, there are a number of viable ways to create music with the six-string bass!

CHAPTER 4
ADDITIONAL TECHNIQUES

Learning all of the notes on a two octave, six-string bass can be a daunting project. I have devised a system that will conceptually teach you a new approach to the chromatic scale, alerting you to a wide variety of note combinations on the neck.

The chromatic scale is a good place to begin memorizing the notes on the neck. Here is a B chromatic scale to acquaint you with the range of the instrument.

Fig. 78

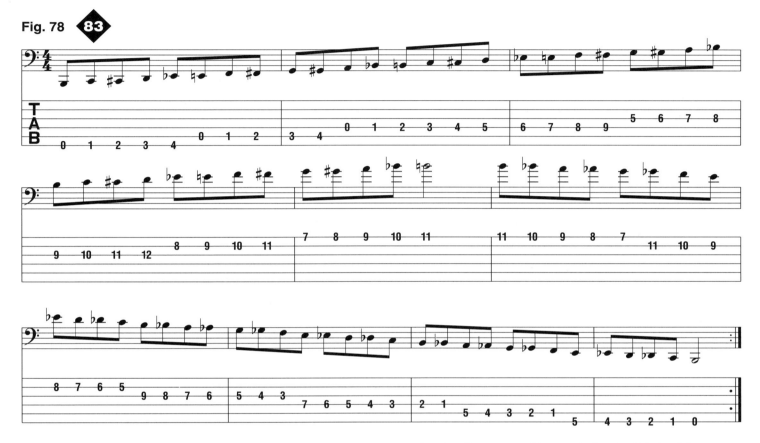

One of my inspirations for the six-string bass is saxophonist, flautist, and bass clarinetist Eric Dolphy. The bass clarinet has a similar range to the six-string bass. Dolphy was an amazing player who would reach into the low depths of the horn and then belt out wild phrases in the high register. This got me thinking about wide intervallic leaps and ways to play them on the bass. This next exercise will help you hear a variety of intervals, play interesting fingerings, and learn the notes on the neck. There are certain ground rules you must adhere to:

- Play these etudes *slowly* until you are confident about the fingerings.
- Transpose them into *all keys.*
- Swing the eighth notes so these etudes can become musical.
- *Have fun with them!*

You may notice some of these lines can be turned into pieces of songs.

Fig. 79

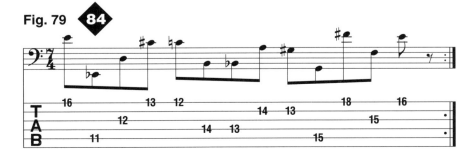

Fig. 80 ◆ **85**

Fig. 81 ◆ **86**

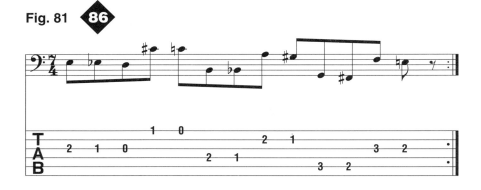

Fig. 82 ◆ **87**

Fig. 83 ◆ **88**

Fig. 84 ◆ **89**

Fig. 85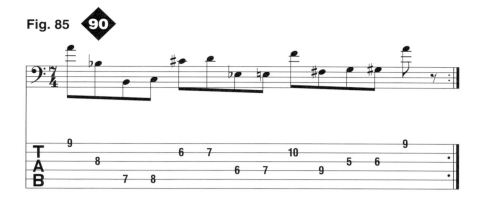

Fig. 86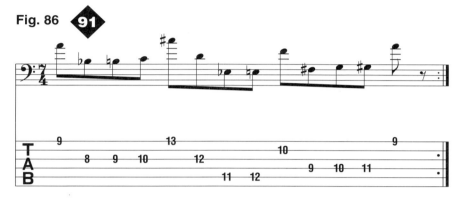

Fig. 87

Fig. 88

Fig. 89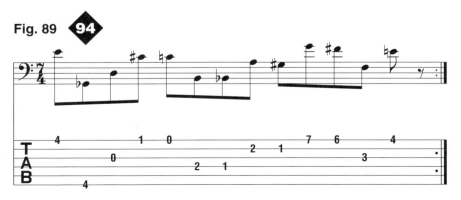

String skipping is another effective way to develop technique and utilize the full range of the instrument. Here is an exercise using a trance-like rhythm along with open strings.

Fig. 90

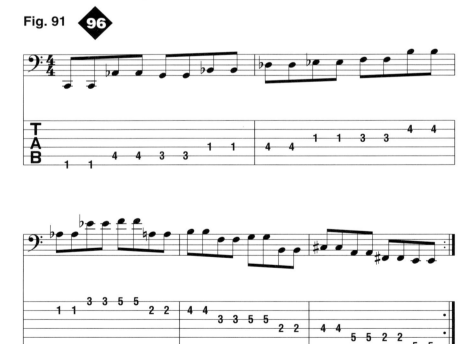

95 cont. Now try playing fig. 95 with the rhythm track.

Try this as an alternative to the previous exercise.

Fig. 91

96 cont. Now try playing fig. 96 with just the rhythm track.

APPENDIX

Additional Scales

This appendix should be used in conjunction with the rest of the book. All the exercises for the major scale and its modes can be applied and *should* be applied to these scales as well. If you want to get more involved with a theory text to supplement this book, refer to my book *The Harmonic Colors for Bass*, which will give you an in depth look at the construction of scales, chords, and melody.

Melodic Minor Scale

Harmonic Minor Scale

Major Blues Scale

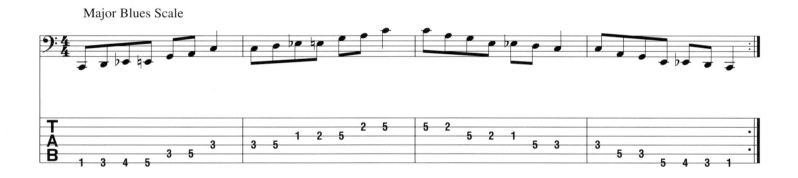

Minor Blues Scale

Altered Blues Scale

Enigmatic Scale

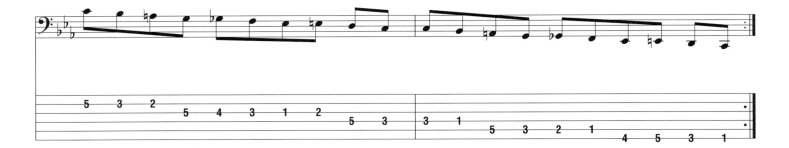

Arabian Scale

Balinese Scale